Phonetic Stories 7

Sight Words
Two Vowels: ēø, āĭ, ēĕ, ōø, īĕ
Silent e • c = s

Raceway Steps 19–20B

MODERN CURRICULUM PRESS
Pearson Learning Group

Contents

A Trip to Sal's

By Sue Dickson

Illustrated by Bob McMahon

Vocabulary Words

1. all
2. any
3. buy
4. come
5. do
6. for
7. go
8. here
9. like
10. look
11. love
12. many
13. me
14. new
15. no
16. one
17. our
18. seconds
19. see
20. she
21. so
22. some

23. that

24. three

25. two

26. very

27. we

28. what

29. when

30. would

31. you

Story Words

ap ple
32. apple

ap ples
33. apples

ba na nas
34. bananas

bas ket
35. basket

Lin da
36. Linda

37. may

38. o'clock

39. snacks

40. Sal's

41. with

"Come here, Tom," said
Mom. "Come here, Jim
and Linda!"

"We will all go to Sal's,"
she said. "We will buy
some ham, milk, and eggs.
We can buy some snacks."

"We do not have very many apples," said Jim. "We love apples. May we get some?" he asked.

"Yes, we will buy some apples and bananas," said Mom. "We will go in just three seconds."

"Look!" said Linda.
"See the new snacks!"
"What will we pick?"
asked Jim.

"I like nuts," said Tom.
Mom said, "We can buy
two bags. Get two bags
from the box. Set the two
bags in our basket."

"Do you see apples and
bananas?" asked Mom.

"Yes, I do!" said Linda.
"I see apples and
bananas."

"May I get one apple
for me, one for Jim, and
one for Tom?" asked Linda.
"No," said Mom. "We
will just buy one big bag."

Mom said to Jim, "See if you can get the bananas. Look for six bananas."

"I see six bananas," said Jim, "but one is stuck."

Linda said, "I can help get it."

Mom said to Tom,
"Would you get the eggs?
I would like a box with
six eggs in it."

"I see one," said Tom.
"I will get it."

"Linda, can you get
that can of ham for
me?" asked Mom.

"Yes, I can," said Linda.

"Do you see any milk,
Jim?" asked Mom.

"Yes. I will get some,"
said Jim.

"It is three o'clock, so we must go," said Mom. "We can have some of our snacks when we get back."

The trip to Sal's was a lot of fun!

The End

A Picnic on the Beach
(Part 1)

By Vida Daly
Illustrated by Dan Grant

Vocabulary Words

1. beach
2. beans
3. boat
4. clean
5. cream
6. deep
7. eat
8. green
9. heat
10. keep
11. lean
12. meal
13. meat
14. neat
15. pail
16. peaches
17. pie
18. sail
19. sail boat
    sailboat
20. seats
21. tea
22. teach
23. year

Story Words

24. be
25. Jack
26. pic nic
    picnic
27. sun
28. this
29. your

"It is very hot," Mom said. "We will go to the beach. The heat will not be so bad at the beach."

"Yes, Mom," said Jack and Sis. "We love the beach!"

"You must not go in very deep yet. When you can swim, you can go in deep. This year, Dad and I will teach you to swim," said Mom.

"I will set up the beach umbrella. It will help keep the sun from us," said Dad.

"Here is your pail, Sis," said Mom. "You can fill it with sand."

"Come with me, Sis,"
said Jack. "We can sail
the sailboat. We will
have fun."

"Look!" said Sis. "See
the boat go. See it sail!"
"One, two, three! Go,
sailboat, go!" said Jack.
"A sailboat is a lot
of fun."

"What will we do next?" said Sis.

"We can have our picnic," said Mom. "We have lean meat and green beans."

"We have peaches and cream," Mom said.

"We have tea and pie," said Dad. "Come sit on a mat. We will eat our meal. This will be fun."

"Sis and I will sit on mats," said Jack.

"Mom and Dad sit on seats. One, two beach seats," said Sis.

"Our picnic was fun," said Dad. "Help us clean up the mess. We can clean it up in six seconds. We must keep the beach neat and clean."

The End (Part 1)

A Picnic on the Beach
(Part 2)

By Vida Daly

Illustrated by Dan Grant

Vocabulary Words

1. ears

2. feed

3. feet

4. float

5. leap

   leap frog
6. leapfrog

   sea weed
7. seaweed

8. wait

Story Words

9. gulls

10. jug

11. let's
    let us

12. lots

13. mats

14. OK

15. pack

    un til
16. until

"Let's go up the beach," said Dad.

"We can feed the gulls," said Mom.

"See us do a leapfrog," said Jack. "Sis and I can leapfrog. Look, Mom! Look, Dad! We can do a leapfrog in the sand!"

"What do you see?" asked Mom.

"I see some seaweed," said Sis. "Look! Lots of green seaweed is on the beach."

"The sand is hot," said Jack. "The sand is very hot for my feet."

"You can get your feet wet," said Mom, "but do not go very deep."

"Will you teach us to swim?" asked Sis.

"Not just yet," said Mom. "We must wait. We cannot swim until three o'clock. We just had our meal."

"OK!" said Mom. "Get set! It is three o'clock! We can leap in! One, two, three, leap in! Leap in, Dad! Leap in, Sis! Leap in, Jack!"

Mom and Dad will
teach Sis and Jack
to swim.

"Kick your feet," said
Mom. "Kick, and kick,
and kick!"

"See Dad float. Dad can float on his back!" said Mom.

"Teach me to float, Dad," said Jack.

"Keep your feet up," said Dad, "and let your ears get wet. Your feet must be up, and your ears must be in! You can float, Jack!"

"We must go," said
Mom. "Help us pack."

Dad will get the umbrella
and the beach seats. Jack
will get the mats and the
sailboat. Sis will get the
jug. Mom will get the
basket and the bag.

"We had fun at the beach," said Sis.

"Yes, the beach is fun when the heat is bad," said Mom.

The End (Part 2)

The Hike
(Part 1)

By Vida Daly
Illustrated by Elizabeth Allen

Vocabulary Words

1. bake
2. bike
3. bikes
4. cake
5. five
6. hike
7. home
8. hope
9. Jake
10. made
11. make
12. Mike
13. pile
14. pine
15. rake
16. take
17. team
18. time
19. tree
20. wave

Story Words

21. by
22. Dan's
23. good-bye
24. grass
25. Jan
26. my
27. could (o͝o)
28. won (wŭn)

"Would you like to go on a hike, Mike?" asked Jake. "We could take our bikes."

"Yes," said Mike. "I will ask my mom and dad if I may go."

"Yes, you may go on a hike with Jake," said Dad.

"Take your bike, but be home at six o'clock," said Mom. "We will eat our meal, and we will have a cake for Dan. Dan's swim team won. Be back at six o'clock."

"OK," said Mike. "We will be back on time. Good-bye!"

"Wave to Mike and Jake, Jan," said Dad. "They will be back at six o'clock."

Dad likes to bake. Dad
will make the cake for
Dan. He will bake a big
cake. Jan went with Dad.
She will help Dad make
the cake.

Mom likes to rake. Mom went to rake the grass. She made a big pile next to the pine tree. "I hope I can get the pile in this bag," said Mom. "I want it neat by five o'clock."

The End (Part 1)

The Hike
(Part 2)

By Vida Daly

Illustrated by Elizabeth Allen

Vocabulary Words

1. bet
2. brain
3. chase
4. creep
5. cried
6. cute
7. fine
8. goat
9. hear
10. need
11. peach
12. rode
13. shade
14. snail
15. soak
16. spoke
17. weed

Story Words

18. duck
19. gift
20. its

Jake and Mike had a fine hike. Jake rode his red bike and Mike rode his green bike. They rode up a hill and had a rest in the shade. They sat by a pond. Mike stuck his feet in the pond to soak.

Jake said, "Look at that cute little duck."

"Yes, I see it," said Mike. "Do you see that bee by the peach tree?"

"Yes," said Jake. "Keep still! See that snail creep up that weed? Look at the little robin in the tree!"

Just as Jake spoke, Mike cried, "Look! A goat! I can hear the bell on its neck!"

"The goat with the bell did not scare the little robin," said Jake. "You did!"

"I would like to get a gift for Dan," said Mike. All at once, Mike could see a little frog hop up on a rock.

"I will creep up and get that frog," said Mike. "A little green frog will be a fine gift for Dan. He will like it."

"Wait," said Jake. "My brain tells me what we need to do. We can get that frog if we chase him fast. The frog must not get to that boat. One, two, three, leap! We got him!"

Mike kept the little
green frog in his pocket.
It was time to go
home, so Mike and Jake
rode fast.

Dan did like his cake, and he did like his little green frog.

"Thank you, Mike," said Dan. "Let's take 'Leap' back to the pond. He will like it best in the pond."

The End

Dave and the Bee

By Sue Dickson

Illustrated by Mike Reed

Vocabulary Words

1. bite
2. came
3. cone
4. Dave
5. drove
6. Duke
7. ear
8. east
9. feel
10. Gail
11. mile
12. name
13. nose
14. road
15. smile

16. tail
17. trail
18. vote
19. Zeke

Story Words

20. are
21. Dave's
22. jumped
23. near
24. pink
25. rab bit
    rabbit
26. rab bits
    rabbits
27. vet

Gail has three rabbits.
Her rabbits are Duke,
Dave, and Zeke.

Duke has a black spot
on his left ear. Dave has a
big pink nose. Zeke has a
tail like a big puff of fuzz.

Dave was in the shade
on a trail. He was near
a pine tree when a pine
cone fell on him. Dave
jumped. A bee was near
Dave. The bee bit Dave
on his nose.

Gail cried, "Help, Mom! Dave has a bee bite on his nose!"

"I will see if the vet has time to help Dave," said Mom.

"The vet can see Dave
at ten o'clock," said Mom.
"Let's get Dave to the vet."

Mom drove to the vet. From home, Mom drove east a mile on Pine Road. Mom drove on Beach Road next to get to the vet.

"Here is our rabbit. His name is Dave," said Mom. "Dave got a bee bite on his nose. The vet said she would see Dave at ten o'clock."

"You must wait. The
vet will see you in just
a little bit," said the
man with a smile.

The vet came in and
said, "Let's take a look
at Dave."

The vet could see a
bump from the bee bite.
The vet could feel the
bump on Dave's nose.

She said, "Dave will feel
fine in time. Just keep the
bite clean."

"Fine," said Mom. "Gail and I can keep it clean so Dave will feel well."

"I vote for that," said Gail.

"Fine," said the vet.

The End

A Visit from Uncle Bruce

By Hetty Hubbard

Illustrated by Sachiko Yoshikawa

Step 20B • Words with **c = s**

Vocabulary Words

1. Bruce
2. dice
3. face
4. Grace
5. ice
6. lace
7. nice
8. place
9. price
10. race
11. rice
12. slice
13. space
14. spice
15. trace
16. twice
17. Vince

Story Words

18. car rots
    carrots
19. comes
20. hap py
    happy
21. Joe
22. liked

23. likes

24. smells

ta ble
25. table

26. then

un cle
27. uncle

28. use

29. visit

30. yelled

yip pee
31. yippee

"Mmmm," said Grace. "That ham with spice smells nice, Mom. When will we eat?"

"Not until six o'clock," said Mom.

"When will you ice the cake? I would like a slice," said Grace.

"Not just yet, Grace," said Mom. "You will have to wait until Uncle Bruce gets here. We will slice the ham and cut the cake when he comes."

"Let me help you get set," said Grace.

"That will be nice, Grace," said Mom. "We can get set twice as fast. Here, you can help Dad dice the carrots. I will do the rice and green beans," said Mom.

Grace has a happy face.
She likes to help. Next,
she will clean the rug.
She gets it nice and clean.

"I will get Joe to help,"
said Grace. "We can have
a race."

Joe and Grace had a
race to dust and wax.
At last, not a trace of
dust was in the place!

"Mom likes this lace
one," said Grace. "Help me
place it on the table, Joe."

Just then Vince came home. He held a nest in his hand.

"Mom, Dad, see what I have!" he said.

"That is nice, Vince," said Mom, "but you must place it back in the tree."

Vince was back fast.
"Let me help you," he
said. "What can I do?"

"You are nice, Vince,"
said Mom. "Ask Dad if he
can use your help."

"You can buy the ice cream," said Dad. "Just tell me the price when you get back."

"Mmm," said Vince. "I like ice cream!"

When Vince came back,
Dad said, "What a big
help you all are."

"Uncle Bruce will like
our place," said Joe.

"Yes," said Grace.

"He will love the ham and green beans," said Grace.

"He will like the carrots and rice," said Dad.

"Uncle Bruce will like the cake," said Mom.

So will I," said Joe. "I have lots of space for it!"

"Uncle Bruce is here!"
said Vince.

"Yippee!" yelled Joe and
Grace. "We can eat
at last!"

The End